Fallen Satori

John D Robinson

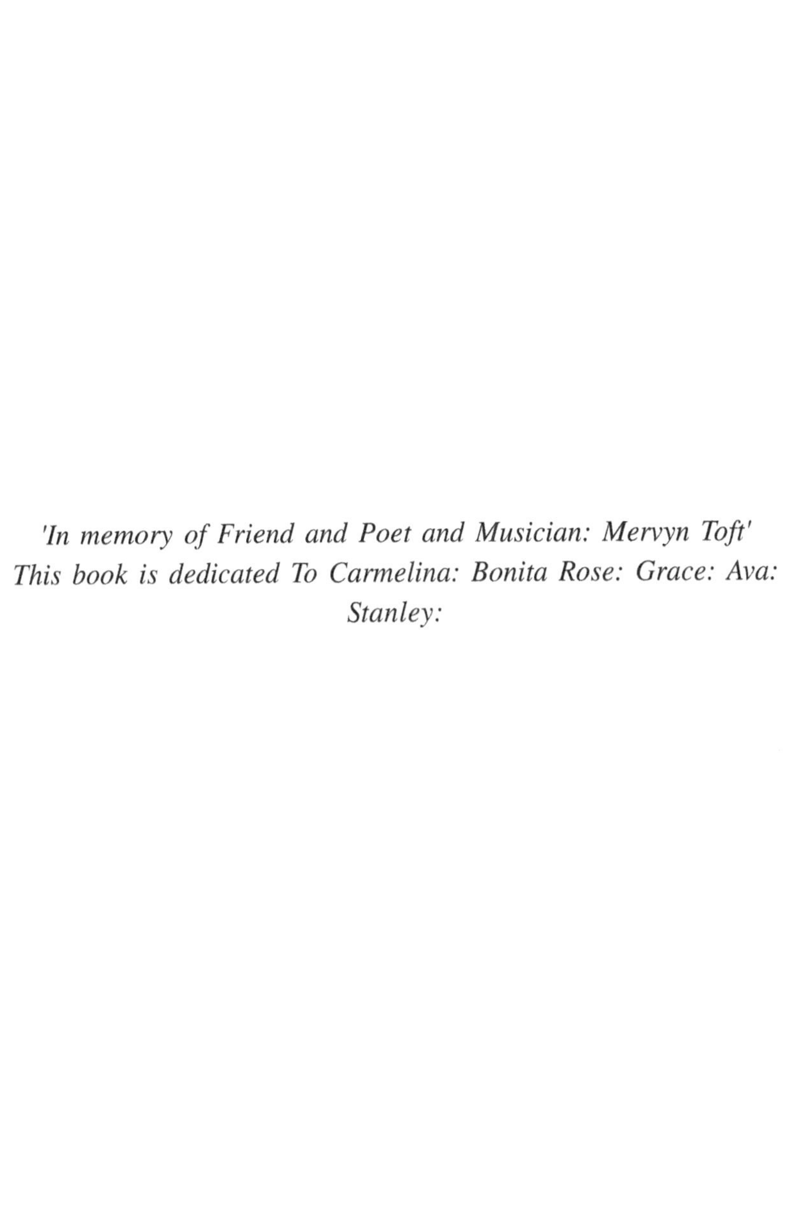

'In memory of Friend and Poet and Musician: Mervyn Toft'
This book is dedicated To Carmelina: Bonita Rose: Grace: Ava:
Stanley:

THE AUTHOR

John D Robinson is a UK poet: hundreds of his poems have appeared online and in print: he has published numerous chapbooks and collections of his poetry: his work is included in countless anthologies: he has been nominated for a 'Pushcart Prize' on two occasions:

'When You Hear The Bell, There's Nowhere To Hide' Holy&intoxicated Publications 2016 (UK) sold out

'Cowboy Hats & Railways' Scars Publications 2016 (USA)

'An Outlaw In The Making' Scars Publications 2017 (USA)

'Hitting Home' Iron Lung Press 2018 (USA) sold out

'The Pursuit Of Shadows' Analog Submission Press 2018 (UK) sold out

'Too Many Drinks Ago' Paper and Ink Press (UK) 2018 sold out

'Echoes Of Diablo' Concrete Meat Press (UK) 2018 sold out

'Pushing Away The Hours' Alien Buddha Press (USA) 2018

'Hang In There' Uncollected Press (USA) 2019

'Singing Aria's' Analog Submission Press (UK) 2019 (sold out)

'A Hash Smoking, Codeine Swallowing, Wine Drinking Son Of A Bitch' 2019 Alien Buddha Press (USA)

'Romance, Renegades & Riots' Analog Submission Press: UK 2019 sold out

'The Sounds Of Samsara' Cyberwit Publishing: (India) February 2020

Sharks and Butterflies 'Cajun Mutt Press) USA Feb/March 2020

3 Poets Series: East London Press (UK) March/April 2020 sold out

'Red Dance' (Uncollected Press USA) March/April 2020

'Smoking Herb and other Stories' Analog Submission Press (UK) April 2020 sold out

'The Dirty Sacrifice & Other Stories' Alien Buddha Press 2020 (USA)

'The Barbed and The Beautiful' Dutch Press with Marcel Herms: The Netherlands 2020

Poems-For-All – Mini books series

'Always More' New & Selected Poems: Horror Sleaze Trash: USA 2020

'A Gallon Of Red, A Gallon Of White' (split with Pete Donohue) Scumbag Press: UK (sold out) 2021

'Still Time': Between Shadows Press: USA: 2021 sold out

'The Songs of Bastet' Scumbag Press UK November 2021 sold out

'The Absence & other Poems' Laughing Ronin Press USA December 2021

'Everyday, Somewhere' Hickathrift Press: UK June 2022

'Running Colours' a novel of fiction Alien Buddha Press 2020

'The Dirty Sacrifice & other stories' Alien Buddha Press 2021

FAT DAVE

He was the one who hung on
the edges of our group
friendship, who followed six
steps behind, who just didn't
quite fit-in with the regulars:
he was fat, he couldn't
play soccer, hit on the girls
or hold his beer: we
considered Fat Dave to be an
asshole loser, an outsider
that went on to own a large
chain of hotels and
restaurants and holiday
resorts as the rest of us
toil and toil and fuck
ourselves up day after
fucking day as Fat Dave
lounges on some fucking
sun-drenched island in
the Mediterranean, as the
rumour constantly
has it, well,
Fuck Fat Dave.

LUSCIOUS LANDLADY

Alcoholic passion had us
wildly embracing and
kissing with abandon, our
hands wandering freely,
our gasps hot and
frequent:
she was my landlady and
lived in the apartment
above mine and then she
forcefully, pushed me away:
'My husband is watching us
from the lounge window,
I'm going to slap your face'
she whispered:
it felt more like a punch,
then her old man was
standing over me with
clenched fists and a vile
mouth and a few days
later I was given a
notice of eviction.

CRETE

That time I was alone and lost
in Crete, wandering around in
the devilish heat, not knowing
where the fuck I was and
knowing I had about an hour
to get back to the arranged
meeting point in town: I was
fucked: I was in a massive
built-up neighbourhood
where the apartment blocks
and streets never seem to
differ: I knelt down to take a
breather and this emancipated,
starving and dying 3 month
old ginger kitten came toward
me: I reached out and stroked
his flea-bitten head and then
picked him up and petted him
as he gently purred best he
could: I put him back down
and he swaggered, tiredly
away to that awaiting time:
I was then convinced that I'd
be wandering these fucking
streets for years, just like the
little kitten and will
perish on a public lawn and
then I heard the most wonderful
of screeches and I looked up

ahead to see the tourist guide,
furiously waving her arms and
with a smile that was thankful
and bitter, that she'd found the
asshole that had
wandered off.

SOMETHING I SAID

I can't recall his name
but he had ginger hair,
he was no bigger or
taller than I, but he
was very fucking angry
with something that I'd
said and he was
desperate to kick my ass:
I couldn't back down,
not in front of all the
guys: we moved slowly
in circles, facing and
insulting one another,
just like in school,
but this was the armed
forces:
'Hey! You two fucking
clowns! are you dancing?'
the platoon Corporal
shouted:
we stopped and stood to
attention:
'No Corporal, we were
shadow boxing' the
ginger haired soldier boy
said:
I looked straight ahead, mouth
shut tightly.
'It looked as though you were

fucking ballet dancing, you
soft cunts, now, fall back into
line, NOW!'
we did and we did our dancing
another time
where he kicked my ass
just like I knew he
would.

A HOME FROM HOME

It was a very small, ground floor
furnished room in a three storey
building opposite the park: I was
nervous and he must have been
aware of it:
'It isn't much and most of it, isn't
mine' he said, casting a half-drunk
smile:
my mother had kicked my father's
ass out of the family home because
of his drinking a few months
previous and this was the first
time I had seen him since then:
I was eleven years old:
I looked around the tiny space, it
was sad, it was beaten, the bed,
the table, two chairs and a wardrobe,
overused and abused and it all
looked dead, only the small stack
of pornographic magazines and
the empty wine bottles shined in
some way: there was no cooker:
'How do you cook?' I asked:
'I eat in restaurants and cafes' he
lied to me: so, I lied too and said,
'I like your room dad'
he nodded his head: 'It's time

for you to go, look after your
mum for me' he said
and it was,
my mother was waiting outside
and everything else seemed
so uncertain.

I HEAR

'**I** hear that you were a boxer'
he said to me through broken
and rotten teeth:
there wasn't too much truth
to this and I didn't know where
it had come from:
 I had boxed for a
short while as a 14-15 year
old: I wasn't gifted, I was
aggressive and spirited and
technically stupid:
I had two fights,
lost both by K.O.
'So, you know how to punch, to
hurt someone?' he said:
'Well, not really, certainly not
now' I replied:
he looked disappointed and
looked past me, looking for
something: I nodded and
walked away as he slammed
the door shut, echoing like a
crazed grenade throughout the
corridors of the high-rise block
of poor and sick apartments,
long overdue modernisation.

JUST WHEN YOU THOUGHT YOU'D GOT AWAY FOR THE DAY

Whilst out walking LoLa the dog,
she came briskly walking by, mid
40's, short brunette hair, attractive
features and figure, dressed in a
black mini dress: a few moments
later, I saw her stop and rifle
through her handbag and then
she kneeled on the pavement and
began to empty the bag's contents
onto the concrete, some items
rolled into the road and she
gasped: 'NO! NO!', she began
sobbing gently: 'OH FUCK!
OH FUCK!'
I retrieved the items from the
road and handed them to her:
'My keys, I left my keys behind!'
she said sadly, acknowledging
the fact that she HAD to go back
for them:
'That's a bastard', I said in sentiment
and truth and I walked on, the
dog straining at the lead, wanting
to get back home, just like the rest
of us.

FROM THE ROOM NEXT DOOR

'I never heard that, I heard
that he slept with Marie!'
I heard through the thin
walls of my room: I didn't
know who he was and I
didn't know Marie: I was
laying on my back upon
the bed, looking up at the
rotten ceiling, following
the rotten cracks:
'NO!' a female voice
shrieked: 'I thought that
Marie was gay!'
this was followed by a
chorus of girly laughter:
I switched on the radio
and looked out of the
window that viewed
across the town, I knew
it well:
R.V. Williams
stirred within the room:
I rolled a joint and then
opened the fridge and
pulled a bottle of wine, I
sparked up and uncorked,
it was 10:30 am, it was
Saturday and it was my day
off.

PICTURE OF MY FATHER

He didn't know of literature
or art
or classical music
or jazz music,
he knew nothing
of opera'
of plays
of movies
he had little knowledge
of popular music,
he could barely
read and write,
he never read a book,
he could charm,
he loved and lost,
he was handsome,
he only ever worked
a few legal
tax-paying
jobs and never
for long,
he wasn't a
husband
father
he was a petty
unsuccessful
thief
and street
alcoholic

that even the love
of his wife
and two
children
could not
cork the bottle
to a fucking
reasonable level
of acceptance
and he
remarried and became
sad and he died of
life and alcohol
and his wife's
prescription drugs
at the age of 44,
it was his birthday,
I had been drinking
with him all day
until 6pm, when I
fucked off to a
party as he tried
to rouse his codeine
soaked wife.

THE STABBING

The morning drifted
into my life in a
frenzied stabbing
hangover, each pulse
of my being echoed
in pain,
we looked at each
other,
our eyes wet with
a love
I was slowly killing
with alcohol,
I looked away
and could see
out of the window,
a seagull
lazily floating
upon the unseen
thermals of
invisible wonder,
we held hands for
a short while and
then I silently
cursed my soul
as I walked into
the kitchen for
the first glass of
the day.

GLIDING

She glided
down the
staircase
like a trickle
of holy
water,
she opened
the door:
'Goodbye'
she said,
with no
smile and a
shine in her
eyes I had
never seen
before.

BIG TONY

Tony thought of
himself as a
tough guy,
a gangster,
he wasn't,
he was a
compassionate
soul who had
great artistic
painting talent:
 he smoked
hash, he sold
hash, he spouted
stories
of breaking
kneecaps and
cutting fingers
off, it was all
bullshit, but Tony
believed it,
unfortunately
so did others:
these days the
terrifying
gangland shadow
lives in a nursing
home for people
with dementia and he
will tell you he

has a gun and will
break out of his
prison cell,
any day now.

THE MIRROR

The reflection
of your
walking by
is momentarily
captured in
the glazed leaf
of a dying
flower,
I hold that
now and hear
your
 footsteps
returning,
like
fingernails
scratching
down a
blind mirror.

THROWN

A gathering of
songbirds
sweep-by as she,
masterfully,
unbuttons her
blouse,
I look on
like a man sat in
the electric chair
waiting for the
switch to be
thrown.

IN HER SHORT LIFE

She lived a
chain of sadness
and
sorrow,
there were no
diamond smiles
or eyes of
electric ecstasy,
but what she left
was a spiralling
energetic
sensation of the
beautiful debris
that enriches
the cities of our
minds
with
love.

THE DOWNFALL

Her beauty
was her
downfall,
her
betrayal,
an invitation
to many
promises,
wishes,
dreams,
that would
never arrive,
maybe she
knew this,
that in the
end nothing
really matters,
no matter
how good or
bad things have
been in
life,
if you had
some good kicks
along the way
and if you
loved and
were loved,
well fuck,

no breath
has ever
been
wasted.

ALL ABOUT YOU

This poem is about you,
that is,
how I knew you.
I was familiar with the
gossip and the bullshit
surrounding you,
but, after our
first meeting I knew
for shit sure it was
bollocks, ugly lies:
in an indescribable
way, like nothing
before in my life,
I fell in love with you,
not sexually/physically
or romantically or
lustfully or out of
pity but for your zest
for life, no matter how
humble or repulsive,
was insatiable,
you loved all of life,
you would see things
in others that no one
else could see or feel,
this poem is all about you,
a decade after you left us
to go to a place, where
you had been so close to,
so many times, before.

KATIE IN CALIFORNIA 1970

When she was one year's old her father
moved the baby into the basement,
chaining her hands to a toilet-chair:
she made too much noise: she slept in
a playpen with a top that was locked:
he would violently force feed the
little girl and as she could not
swallow comfortably, she would
vomit and her father would become
enraged and would shout and
scream vileness and would bark
and snarl like a rabid dog and on
countless occasions he would beat
her with a big stick:
mother and two teenage sons
lived in fear, knowing of the
horrors happening below them
every fucking day: after eleven
years, her mother and one of
the son's took the young twelve
year old to hospital: initially
the nurses guessed her to be about
seven or eight years old:
shocked at the girl's physical
appearance and neglect she was
hospitalised: she was unable to
walk or speak, and the
authorities were alerted: the sadistic
asshole father was charged with

severe child abuse and neglect, before
trial, he shot himself through the
head: the mother was judged as a
victim of psychological, bullying,
coercive, threatening, controlling
abusive behaviour: briefly the girl
moved into a State-run children's
home and then was placed into a
family foster home who held
extreme Christian views and values:
one time, when she vomited into a
bowl and then continued to eat,
the foster father hit her hard
across the head and then she
refused to eat as she feared that
would vomit again: she would
self-harm by scratching
her arms repeatedly until they
bled heavily she was then taken
back to hospital and after, she
was given back to the care of her
mother, which lasted just a few
weeks before she returned her back
to the authorities who again
placed her in a children's home.
her days thereafter are unknown
and even fifty years later the
real identities of the little girl and her
parents have not been revealed.

BURN OUT

So many
have tried
to put the
fires out
and
failed,
there was
always
something
remaining
and even
in death,
by way of
dirty heroin,
even that
did not
extinguish
that natural
beauty of
your
wonderful
inferno.

STUDIO WORK

In silence, was I,
smoking a joint of hash,
sat in my studio
and I saw a wasp
entangled in a thick
spider's web,
thrashing, struggling
violently to free
itself to escape
death:
for some moments
I watched nature
working its survival,
capture, kill or be
killed and then I
thought, fuck it,
I didn't know this
wasp and it didn't
know me but that
didn't seem to
matter as I
carefully cut
through the web
with sharp scissors,
the pour soul was
frantic as I moved
outside where I
very gently snipped
away

at the sticky fabric and
then within a few
moments, the wasp
broke free and
flew away, not
looking back:
'Good luck fella'
I whispered,
picking up the joint
and inhaling
healthily
through a
tight smile.

THE BANK ROBBER

Allen was a gentle man,
his I.Q. wasn't high
but his vulnerability was
and his addiction to
speed was legendary:
his sparse, squalid flats
were easily commandeered
by dealers and 'friends'
leading to numerous
evictions and periods of
homelessness:
maybe, early on in his
life, he may have
pursued love, dreams
and the usual heart-breaking
bullshit and found
nothing but disappointment
and amphetamines
and madness and these
became his life:
then one desperate day
he walked into a bank and
handed the cashier, a
hand-scrawled ineligible
note that demanded a sum
of money and that he had
a gun, (which he didn't)
the cashier could not decipher
 the note:

decades of drug abuse and
psychiatric treatments had
robbed Allen of any clarity
of speech, he quickly became
frustrated and walked out of
 the bank to a bus stop to go
home but minutes later a
flood of armed police arrived
and he was brutally
apprehended:
he received a six- year prison
sentence, most of which, he'll
probably spend in the
hospital wing: perhaps not
stable or the safest, not a place
he could call his own, but
somewhere where Allen
could have many freedoms
he had never known.

I WAS TOLD THAT BEING BORN A POET IS

Like looking into
a facial portrait of
a Pasada picture
or like
licking the bones
of centuries that
have been scourged
without mercy,
or like
wearing a death-
mask that welcomes
the coldness with a
wraith of
vile vespers,
or
when even
loneliness
turns away from
you at the most
desperate moment
and your only
hope is the
darkest
of
corners,
I think that's
bullshit,
too soft,
sounds like a

gentle stroll
through the
fucking
park.

IT SLIPS

How it slips
so easily from
joy, ecstasy and
adventurous
exploration
to
mind-numbing
conventional
bullshit of
learned tedious
themes that
hardly keep a
heart beating
let alone pay
the rent,
how this life
seeps slowly,
secretly into a
mundane endless
plot of no-sense,
of a journey
that back-tracks
into itself to
find where it
began and how
the wonder has
been lost to a
sterile
conformity.

AN ANGRY ANDREW

Andy was volatile
angry and aggressive,
he'd had half his
right leg amputated
after using
infected dirty
needles:
'You name it, I've
been addicted to it'
he told me proudly:
'Bullshit' I said:
'Fuck you man! I
mean it, I've shot
everything!' he
snarled back:
'I've no doubt, but
bullshit
is all there is,
we all overdose
on bullshit'
I said coldly:
he looked at me
with prison-eyes,
'Yeah' he said 'You
got something
there'.

THANKFULLY

Rose was not a
regular drinker,
for when she drank
she was ill tempered
and violent:
if some asshole
was getting too
disruptive, Rose
would stop it
quickly and
effectively
with a blow to the
head with a
frying pan,
kettle,
a wooden chair,
rolling pin,
metal tray,
anything at hand:
many troublesome
drunkards carry
a tattoo
gifted from
Rose,
who,
thankfully,
no
longer
drinks.

ON THE WAY UP

When I last saw him
he told me he was
climbing to the stars,
that he was living the
dream, that paradise
was in every breath
and that love could
never be defined
but he was ascending
a stairwell toward a
higher understanding
of being
and he was found
dead in his lonely
room,
with lonely photographs
and lonely possessions
and lonely memories,
just like the breeze,
belonging to no one
but touching us all
even
just for that pure
instant disappearing
moment of
truth.

TAP TAP

The knock on the door
always
comes at the wrong time,
when you're lovemaking
on a sunny Sunday
afternoon,
during a drug-drop when
relatives pay a surprise
visit,
when the post delivery
hands-over a court date
as the landlady hammers
the door for way overdue
rent,
when your new lover drops
by with a surprise bottle of
wine and you're already
fucked-up on narcotics
and your previous lover
is waiting on a call,
when a political or
religious pusher
relentlessly pounds
or when the
season of ghosts and
demons from your past,
rip the door clean
off its hinges,
it's time to throw

away the key and
look out at the
countless shattered
doors
left in
your
wake.

SUCKING AND HITTING

More than many times,
she'd had the choice of
suck dick or no hit
and
when her pockets
were lined, she'd give
it away and would
leave her debt owing
to the dealers, she'd
give her cash to
others that she felt
needed it more than
she and maybe
they did,
she was
extraordinarily
warm and gifted
in many ways
and maybe she was
loved by many
but I could see
her loneliness
trailing her like
like a bullet
in slow motion,
aiming for her
beaten
spirit.

JOANNA, A POEM FOR YOU

It wasn't the
ravages of time
or
the drugs and
alcohol
or
the harshness
of
homelessness
and
loneliness
or
the absence
of affection
or
the violence
of crazed
strangers
that killed
her,
no,
it was
life
that
took
her.

ALL SORTS

Some cling to poetry
like a lifebuoy but
never really getting a
good solid grip,
others dive in and
swim around and
around and around,
some drown,
others parachute,
landing awkwardly
and lose any rhythm,
some desire the
accolade of poet
and become blinded
by it,
others dig tunnels,
never ending tunnels,
some kick-back,
write it down,
get rid and don't
give a fuck,

I love these
poets,
you ask them.

HACKED OFF

Although Mother sun was
high and blazing in blue
and white,
I felt pissed
I felt pissed off
with a lot of things,
with
the horrors of Ukraine
and conflicts around the
world
with
global politics
theology
philosophy
history
art
literature
but I wasn't pissed
at music
or with my
lover
but I was
really pissed off
with
poverty
hunger
homelessness
injustice
with

the seemingly
hopelessness of
getting it right,
with
the bullshit of
talentless millionaires
called celebrities
with
the shadows that cloak
me with the chimes of
sorrow that taint my
soul with kisses of
sweet betrayal,
I felt pissed
not with Mother sun
or even my neighbours,
but finally, I realised, I
was pissed off
with myself
and gave up looking
for the answer to
the songs in
my head.

MORNING NAKED

Feeling her warm morning
nakedness lying beside me
as I awoke
shyly startled me as I
gazed at her beauty for
the first time in
daylight,
I dare not move
and fooled myself
listening to the world
outside, waking up and
trudging another day
of denial
of defeat,
I curled into her skin
and fell
back to sleep.

A GUY CALLED HENRY THAT YOU DIDN'T KNOW

"Give me a kiss!" he said.
"Listen Henry', I said smiling,
'I've a reputation to upkeep
and kissing a drunken gypsy
in a hotel room on a Friday
afternoon could rip it apart;
 besides what would my seniors
at the office think!
HEY! What the fuck
would my wife say?"
"GO ON! GIVE ME A KISS!"
he roared, swaying on his feet,
beer can in hand,
grinning a black toothed,
gold toothed grin.
"It's out of the question Henry', I said
 and then, 'Here, I've brought
you some food"
"YOU DO LOVE ME!"
Henry barked, laughing.
I nodded slowly; I couldn't deny it;
Henry was Roma,
he was a scoundrel
and a husband and father,
a brother and an uncle
and grandfather,
he was a drinker and a gambler
and a friend and enemy to many

and he was one of the most endearing
 and honest of people I have ever met;
he made me laugh and smile
and he provoked me into thinking
and contemplating like few people
 have done and he lived life as it came at him.
Dead now; perhaps nine years;
 heart attack.
Henry wasn't prepared for his end,
the world didn't stop,
not even for a moment
 and he wouldn't have wanted it to.

FORM FILLING

"Have you a partner?" I asked, knowing him well and that he did not.

"Yes I have" he said quickly.

"Oh okay, is this a recent thing? What's her name?" I said.

"It's a he" he said "and it's long term, I mean it for eternity"

"Oh a he!" I said surprised.

"Yeah" he said "Anything wrong with that?"

"No nothing wrong with that" I said, "What's his name?"

"His name?" he asked.

"Yeah, his name" I said.

"Jesus Christ" he said softly, "It's Jesus Christ"

"Jesus Christ!" I said smiling and grinning.

"Yeah" he said seriously looking at me hard.

"They're asking for a date of birth" I said

"Well, everybody knows that! Christmas Day; twenty fifth of December zero zero zero zero!" he answered with confidence.

"Okay" I said "Now they're asking for proof of birth; a birth certificate"

"Fuck me!" he cried "The Bible that's His birth certificate, He's got millions of birth certificates all over the world!"

"Alright" I said "They're being awkward now, they're asking for a national insurance number"

"Jesus don't need no national insurance number; but okay; here's His national insurance number; JC 1" he laughed softly.

"Okay" I said "Now if the authorities take this literally you will lose your single person reduction for your taxes"

"Okay" he said "That's fine; I'll gladly pay for Jesus, I mean, after all man, He paid the ultimate price for us all didn't he?" he looked at me for reassurance.

"Maybe" I said looking away, out of the window and into the distance.

"I'll pay for Jesus" he said. "I'll pay"

ON THE DAY THAT OSCAR LEFT ME

I awoke terribly fragile,
shaking and frightened and
I called in sick,
an ex lover
telephoned and asked
for money
which I didn't have,
the backyard flooded
and my pot dealer
had gone on
holiday,
the radio broadcast
stories of tragedy
and sadness and
of wars
and payday was
two weeks away;
Oscar had suddenly
shown up a few
months back, wailing
and crying and
hungry and we made
friends and he moved
in and I called him
Oscar and he ate
whatever I could
give him and he
seemed thankful and
then one day he

didn't come back
and I
knew that he
wouldn't return;
Oscar was a beat hobo cat;
I had a real lousy
day the day
that Oscar
left me.

THERE'S ALWAYS MORE

Julian was tall and skinny,
too skinny maybe and he
was gentle, articulate, creative
and very effeminate in
his mannerisms and
manners;
when we first met
he was kicking heroin
and for 3 or 4 days
I witnessed his
withdrawal and I held
him and he clung to me
and then he found
God and fell in love
with a friend of mine
who had also recently
been re-born;
they married and
had 2 sons, the marriage
lasted perhaps
several years and
then Julian split with
God and his wife and
children and
found a male lover
and moved from town
to city; his sons
visited a few times

and retuned with
tears and cigarette
burns and bad dreams
and they never saw
their father alive
again and neither
did I.
Later, his lover
died of HIV AIDS
and Julian had
same diagnosis and
he committed
suicide
and I remember Julian
one time telling me
of blowing truck drivers
in midnight deserted
car parks and that
he would've have
done anything for
a needle-push of
heroin but God had
saved him;
there's a lot more
to this story
as there will be
to yours,
but for now,
for Julian,
this will do it.

AS SOON

As I entered the
supermarket I
needed to step
quickly backwards
to make way for
 a sprinting
and laughing
teenager
with a hand-basket
full of groceries
in one hand and
clutched beneath his
other arm
a small baby;
that was bobbling
around and laughing
and having a
good time,
following very close
behind was another
 laughing, sprinting
young guy;
he didn't have a baby
but had a hand-basket
in each hand, full of
beer and groceries.
The fat security guard
waddled very slowly
towards the exit/entrance

and stepped out into
the street,
he lazily swung his head
left and right
and then shrugged his
sagging shoulders and
frowned and said to
no one
"They've got away"
and then he
wobbled back into
the store;
"I'll have to phone this
in and then write it up;
it's gonna take me
some time"
and then he ambled
out of sight
towards the back of
the store;
I stepped back in
and looked over at
a grinning cashier;
"Your security
Is tight" I said.
The cashier smiled
and then shaking
his head said,
 "Yeah, tighter than
Mother Teresa"
Leaving the store
I thought of the
baby,

now a potential
felon, an accessory
to robbery,
running away
in fear of capture
before he could
even walk into the
arms of his poor
mama.

IT WAS AMONGST

One of the most dumbest
things I have ever done in
my life;
I knew it was dumb
but I couldn't stop myself
and as I over-took the
motorcycle cop on the
inside, I thought to
myself 'This is a fucking
dumb thing to be doing'
within moments the cop
was passing me and
gesturing me to pull-over;
I glided the Yamaha over
to the road-side, killed the
engine, parked and walked
over to where he stood;
"Take off your helmet"
he said
I did so without question
and said
"Listen officer, that was
stupid what I just did"
my breath hit him hard
and his face grimaced
and he asked
"Have you been drinking?"
"Not this morning officer" I said
"That doesn't humour me,

when did you take your last
drink?"
"About 9pm last night" I lied
"And how much did you drink?"
he asked,
"Two glasses of wine" I lied
"Smells like 2 bottles of wine"
he said,
how the fuck did he know?
I thought to myself.
"You're lucky, I don't have
the breathalysing kit. What you
just did was idiotic, it was
just plain dumb, are you dumb?"
he asked.
"I guess so" I said
"Where are you going?" he said
"To work" I said.
"Okay, go on, I'll be
watching you" he said
waving me away.
I climbed back onto the
machine and pulled away
into the creeping
lines of traffic and
looked into the mirrors
and watched as the cop
got smaller and smaller
and when he vanished
from view, I opened up
the throttle; being late
for work 2 days in a
row wasn't going to
look good.

ONE OF THE FAMILY

A few weeks previous
I had seen him, staggering,
falling and crashing
head-first into a parked
car and then laying upon
the cold concrete and
cursing and shouting and
then laughing as he
gathered himself upright,
blood trickled from his
head and he lurched
forward; all the while
muttering and whispering
to himself;
I crossed the road to
avoid any contact and I
hurt myself to do so;
a university educated guy,
we had many literary
discussions and he always
told me 'Read Faulkner,'
which I never did;
he worked hard and had
married in the university
town, raised children and
bought homes and cars and
then it all went wrong; I never
did find out what but he
returned to his home-town

and committed himself
to alcohol; he married a
simple woman and fathered
3 children and very
occasionally I would visit
the family home and
drink with him;
he'd sit and sleep in an
armchair in the lounge;
beside the chair was a fridge;
he never slept for more than
2 or 3 hours at a time,
he'd awake and open the
fridge door and pull out
a can; the tv was always
on silent; flickering;
something to stare at
in the early hours; the
house was sparse, naked
of comfort or
friendliness or attraction
but home for 3
young lives; following the
breakdown of this marriage
he lived alone in rented
rooms and was evicted
again and again until
no landlord would
accept him and he ended
up on the streets;
he was in his early
50's and
was found frozen to

death one
February morning in
a seaside alleyway;
I never made his funeral
and I know for shit-sure
that he won't make mine.

9 789395 224284